MOMMA'S LAST BREATH

By

Yevette Fisher

Copyright ©2019
By Globe Shakers, LLC

This book or parts thereof may not be reproduced in any form, stored in a retrieval system, or transmitted in any form; electronic, mechanical, photocopy, recording, or otherwise is not permitted without prior written permission of the authors.

ISBN 978-0-9997545-8-0
©2019

All rights reserved

Printed in the United States of America

Names have been changed to use discretion

Online store/contact info www.globeshakers.com

Other Suggested Reads

Devil Let My Baby Go
Yevette Fisher

Walk by Faith Prayer Journal
Yevette Fisher

Shop online @   globeshakers.com

Covenant Gear Christian Rainbow Apparel

Table of Contents

The Retreat 1

Jesus Worked It Out 11

On A Mission 16

Shifting Gears 24

God Speaks.. 28

Last Ride Home 41

Bye Bye Momma....................................... 48

Momma's Last Breath 55

The Arrangements 62

A Friend To The Rescue 74

Warfare 82

Family Feud 87

Laid To Rest.. 91

Sweet Memories.. 99

Reflections Of Our Bond 110

Words Of Encouragement.................... 118

Momma's Legacy 124

Foreword

Momma's Last Breath candidly discusses real life situations that everyone can relate to when facing sorrowful moments. The author, Yevette Fisher's submission to God is evident in the midst of tragedy. This book will encourage readers to pray and seek God's voice when everything looks grim. While dealing with grief, this certainly uplifts, comforts, and provides great advice to heal.

Vanessa Galvin

Lera Reid-Fisher

The Retreat

I was having a wonderful time in the Lord at a women's retreat hosted by my church. We were at a beautiful resort in Palm Springs, California. The Sonoran Desert climate was extremely hot and humid. The city is known for its hot springs, stylish hotels, golf courses, and spas. It was in the month of August. As we gathered inside the air-conditioned conference room, praises rang throughout the atmosphere. There were approximately one hundred and fifty women that attended the retreat that year.

As we were enjoying the worship and fellowship, I received a phone call. I walked out into the hallway to answer my cell phone. My niece, Tanesha sounded like she was in tears on the other end.

"What's wrong Tanesha?" I asked.

"The doctors said grandma has cancer and it's stage 4, and there is nothing they can do for her," she said, hysterically.
"Calm down baby, Grandma is going to be alright. I'm not receiving that report; God is a healer! I am going to believe the report of the Lord. The name of Jesus is bigger than cancer," I said, with assurance."

Due to being at the retreat, I was feeling spiritually empowered. I had been in a season of fasting and prayer. Immediately, I started to pray for my sweet niece. She was a freshman at Paine College staying on campus in Augusta, Georgia. As I was talking, one of the Evangelist walking through the hall overheard me.
"Is everything okay?" she asked.
"This is my niece on the phone, and she just told me that my mother has been diagnosed with stage 4 colon cancer," I explained.
"Oh no!" she replied.

The Evangelist went to gather a few more sisters to come out of the mid-day service. I called Momma at the hospital in Atlanta. The operator put the call through to her room.

"Hello," Momma answered.
"Praise the Lord! How are you Momma?" I asked.
"I'm fine baby," she said, softly.

Normally Momma and I were upbeat and laughing before we could even get into our conversation. Not this time. This was a different type of call. We both were very sober. My mother was full of the Holy Ghost, and a firm believer that God answers prayers. She sounded strong. I could tell Momma was happy to hear my voice.

"I just received a phone call from Tanesha she informed me that the doctor diagnosed you with stage 4 cancer," I explained.

"Yes, that's what they told me," she said, calmly.

Momma took a deep breath and sighed.

"I am here in Palm Springs at a women's retreat surrounded by some of the sisters. We are going to pray for you and believe God for your healing," I expressed.

"Okay baby," she said, gratefully.

There was about five of us out in the hallway. As we formed a circle, I placed my cell phone in the middle of the table. We began to corporately intercede for my mother and called on the name of Jesus. We fervently prayed, exercising great "faith."

"I love you Momma; I'll be making plans to fly to Atlanta as soon as I return home."

"Alright shugga, I will talk to you later," she said.

"Bye, bye." I thought to myself, 'I wish I was right there with Momma.'

I was appreciative that my niece Tanesha called to inform me of the situation. I was not nervous or fearful. I strongly felt this would be an opportunity for God to get the glory out of the circumstances. Tanesha was more like a daughter to Momma than a grandchild. My mother raised her since she was five, because my sister was addicted to drugs.

The Women's President of my church was also included in the prayer for Momma. We went back into the service. She announced the news I received and asked if all the women would come into agreement for my mother's healing. The power of God was present in that room. I began to praise and worship God with passion.

The kind of anointing that was present was indescribable. A radical breakout of praise fell in that room. We were literally running around as we declared healing for Momma in the name of Jesus! Sisters were giving testimonies about family members that had been healed from cancer. It was explosive! Some of the praise leaders started singing too.

I ran several laps around that conference room as an act of faith. I was trusting in God to heal my mother with a victorious outcome. Then, all the women were hugging, crying, and praying for me. Some laid hands on me and spoke words of encouragement. I will never forget that moment. Little did I know, God was strengthening me for the journey ahead. The power of God was supernaturally resting upon me.

As I reflect, before attending the retreat a week prior, one of the Evangelists named Mae approached me after Sunday morning service. She asked to speak with me briefly. "Are you going to the women's retreat Sister Yevette?" she asked.

"No, I was not planning to go this year. I have a family reunion the same week of the retreat," I replied.

"Well, I am not going to be able to go to the retreat and I've already paid in full. The Lord told me to give the retreat package to you," Evangelist Mae said.

"Are you sure?" I asked.

She sharply rebuked me.

"I know God's voice. He told me to give my place to you," she said, with an attitude.

Evangelist Mae operated in some prophetic gifts but tended to get agitated when you seemed skeptical of her ability to hear from God. Her response almost caused me to decline her offer. She seemed annoyed that I questioned her. I was not one who took advantage of people, so I wanted to be sure that she was instructed by God to bless me.

"I will pray and get back with you," I replied.

"Okay, well let me know what you decide," Evangelist Mae said.

I had been in attendance for the past 10 years at the women's retreat. Initially, for whatever reason, I wasn't feeling it this year. My family on my Father's side was having a reunion in our hometown Oceanside, California. Some of my cousins asked me to be the Chaplain that year. I didn't feel led to go to the reunion either because my unsaved family members liked to debate biblical differences.

Shortly after talking to Evangelist Mae, I went back into the sanctuary to pray at the altar. The Lord instructed me to go to the women's retreat and gave me a peace about it. I saw Evangelist Mae before night service that evening and told her that I would accept her offer.

"Thank you so much, for considering me. God has led me to go," I said.

"You're welcome," she replied, with a smile.

She was relieved that I accepted the invitation. There was a meeting for the retreat attendees in the fellowship hall just before evening service. I went to the meeting to gather all the details. Evangelist Mae informed the Women's President that I was going in her stead.

This was preparation for what was ahead. God's timing is impeccable! I thank the Lord that I decided to go that year. I was walking in an unusual anointing upon my return from the retreat. My faith in God was unshakeable. I truly reverenced the word of God, and always tried to live holy while trusting God in every circumstance.

While on the retreat: we fasted, prayed, and worshipped the Lord. We started off with a 6 AM prayer clinic. Then, we had workshops, lunch, leisure time, and more services. There were a variety of speakers that taught the Word of God.

Each of us shared a room with a sister from the church. This gave us the chance to get to know each other on a more personal level. Being at the retreat was more of an intimate setting. The curriculum allowed us to also vent and lay down our heavy burdens dealing with life's issues. It was a time to reflect on ourselves and evaluate our relationship with God. It was a spiritual vacation away from the routine of life.

On Sunday morning, we all returned directly to the church on a charter bus. We marched into the sanctuary with unity and power. The Women's Auxiliary called our experience, "The Mountain Top." We returned feeling fortified.

There was an excitement when the bus pulled up to the church. Everyone that did not go on the retreat, rushed to get a seat to join the celebration. All the women exited the bus with their white outfits on. We lined up in pairs to make our victorious entrance.

The seats were roped off for those of us that were marching in. We had rehearsed at the retreat. The ushers held the double doors open as we came in singing our theme song. I sang in the choir that day too. We rejoiced as Pastor delivered a powerful message. Though it was exciting, my mind was on Momma's diagnosis.

During the altar call, I was praying for people. Afterwards, I interceded with baptism candidates that desired to be filled with the Holy Spirit. I went to get something to eat and rested in our lounge until evening service started. Every Sunday, I followed the same routine as a faithful servant. Even though I was enjoying the day, Momma was heavy in my spirit. That night, I arrived home late and began to make arrangements to fly to Atlanta.

Jesus Worked it Out

The next morning, I called my Pastor to let him know that my Mother was severely ill. Technically, he was Momma's Pastor as well. She got saved at my church twenty years prior, while visiting me for Mother's Day.

"Praise the Lord Pastor, I received a call while I was at the retreat that Momma was diagnosed with stage 4 cancer. I don't have the money to get to Atlanta, and I was wondering if you could help me?" I explained.

"Absolutely, Sister Yevette just let me know how much you need, and I'll have the church secretary write you a check by tomorrow," Pastor said, genuinely.

"Thank you so much Pastor I appreciate it." I said, with gratitude.

These sorts of difficult times made me thankful for a stable ministry. The church was an emotional support system. I had been a dedicated member for over 25 years. I had a good rapport with my pastor. I shared the Gospel with hundreds of people through Outreach Ministry. The majority of my family, and many of my friends had been baptized in the name of Jesus Christ and filled with the Holy Spirit at my church.

I had worked on several auxiliaries and was a weekly tither for twenty years. Pastor had given me wise counsel on some occasions. He also financially assisted my family during their dilemmas. He never hesitated when I came to him for help. Pastor was like a Father figure. I was grateful to God that he was willing to help me get my ticket to Atlanta.

That was a rough era. There were 3 others at my church who lost a parent in that same week. All the bereaved were close to me. I was the only one that had to travel out of town to see about my mother. I remember Bernie Mac the actor/comedian died also. I was in the bank preparing to go to see about Momma and overheard a woman on her cell phone as I used the ATM machine. I could hear bits of conversations going on.

"What! Bernie Mac died!" I overheard someone say.

Then another person mumbled with surprise, "What, I didn't know he was sick."

"Excuse me," I said, as I interrupted their conversation. "Did you say that Bernie Mac died?"

"Yes," the stranger replied.

I felt a sadness. The feeling you get when you have watched a celebrity on television for years and they remind you of your own family. As I faced my own crisis, now one of my favorite actors passed. Even today, when I see an old Bernie Mac movie my mind immediately reflects back to that day. It's kind of like, when you smell a certain scent, perfume, or a flower, and it makes you think of a moment in your life.

I was praying for an inexpensive fare, as I sat at the computer trying to find a flight to Atlanta. I received a phone call from my good friend Laura. She often passed my house in route to her business. Laura was aware of the situation with my mother and was calling to check on me.

"Praise the Lord, what are you up to?" Laura asked.

"Praise the Lord girl, I'm trying to make arrangements to leave. I found a reasonable price, but I've got to go pick up a check from Pastor at the church," I answered.

"My God, I was driving down the street, and the Lord said, 'Call Yevette to see if there's anything she needs.' I have five hundred dollars on me right now, so I want you to go ahead and buy your ticket before the price increases," Laura said.

"Awww, Laura thank you!" I replied, endearingly.

My friend Laura and her husband were financially blessed. They were not selfish people, and often helped others that were less fortunate. Laura and I were very close and supported one another during difficult times. God was moving like clockwork!

She swiftly pulled up in front of my house. We went to the bank and deposited the money to purchase the ticket. I booked the flight. She drove me to the church to pick up the check that our Pastor was giving me. Laura insisted that she did not want to be reimbursed, and to use what Pastor helped me with for travel expenses. I was in tears for gratitude of what God was doing. "Thank you so much Laura," I said gratefully. The Lord was working on my behalf.

~ God is faithful. ~

On a Mission

The next day, my friend Laura dropped me off at the airport. I was praying during the entire flight to Atlanta, and still believing God for Momma's divine healing. My Prayer Shawl, and Blessed Oil were in my purse. I believed Momma was coming out of the hospital healed and whole. God was keeping me in perfect peace (Isaiah 26:3). There was a level of spiritual authority that seemed to be resting upon me for this trip. I was spiritually equipped through fasting and prayer.

My niece Tanesha was two hours away from Atlanta taking her finals at Paine College. She made arrangements with Momma's neighbors across the street to pick me up. The MARTA train passed through the airport terminals, and my transit stop was a few blocks away. The neighbors had the house/car keys, so that I could drive myself to the hospital.

As I walked into Momma's house, there was a basin turned over with a towel in front of her favorite chair. Dishes with food in them were left on the dining room table. It was apparent she was quite ill. I felt sad that Momma did not call to make me aware that she was suffering. We talked every day, and not once did she mention being in any type of pain.

Reflecting on our last few conversations, Momma seemed to be in a hurry to end the call. We always had our regular morning prayer and coffee over the phone. It was beginning to seem a little odd, "my mother" wanted to end our conversation in less than an hour. Her pattern was subtly changing.

I was on a mission to see about Momma despite coming off a 5-hour flight. Before heading out, I took a moment to kneel in prayer, and anoint my forehead with Blessed Oil. I drove her car downtown to Grady Hospital. Atlanta's weather was scorching hot in August too.

I was relieved to finally be there. As I approached the elevator, I couldn't wait to see Momma. I walked into her room and she was resting in the hospital bed. Momma's face lit up! She was glad to see me. I noticed a weight lift off of her as if her worries were over.

"Hey baby," she said, sweetly.

"Hi Momma," I said, with a sigh of relief.

I went over and kissed her forehead as I wrapped my arms around her.

"How do you feel Momma."

"I'm fine, as well as could be expected," she said.

We engaged in a little small talk, then I did not waste any more time. Immediately, I took my Prayer Shawl, and my Blessed Oil out of my purse. My mother was a sanctified believer and was familiar with these sacred items. I began to read scriptures to Momma. Then, I rubbed her body down in the anointing oil while praying with great faith.

It was such a comfort to be there with her. My mother knew she would be taken good care of now. There was a sense of security that I felt between the two of us. I was her first daughter, which caused us to have an incredible bond. As the third oldest child out of eleven, she raised me to be responsible. In addition to being mother and daughter, we were friends. She affectionately gave me the nickname "Becky."

Shortly after, the doctor entered the room to check on Momma. She was a chubby, short woman, with a caramel complexion, and pretty smile.

"Hi, I'm Dr. Williams. Who is going to be in charge if we need any information?" she asked.

"This is my daughter Yevette, she's in charge," Momma said.

"I need to meet with all your children to go over your diagnosis. When is a good time?" Dr, Williams asked.

"Tomorrow is good," Momma replied.

There were 3 other siblings residing in Atlanta. I contacted them, and they planned to come to this meeting at the hospital the next day. 'Visiting hours are over,' the intercom announced. I hugged Momma, kissed her gently, and assured her I would be back tomorrow.

I went back to Momma's house and prayed all night. I wanted to stay in a consecrated mindset, so I could hear from God. I was believing a miraculous healing would manifest for Momma. I wondered, 'Was I going to have to move to Atlanta, or was this going to be an instant manifestation?' There was no doubt in my mind that Momma was not going to be healed! Some people in the Bible were healed as time progressed.

The next day, I got to the hospital early. My sister Denise was already there with her boyfriend Freddie. My youngest brother, Vernell came after them. Dr. Williams came to the meeting with a half dozen other physicians accompanying her. It was impressive that these women were African Americans. I had never seen a whole medical team that was black.

I had to ask some visitors to please excuse themselves. My brother Vernell thought I was rude. I did not know those people, and I felt only immediate family needed to be present for this personal meeting with the doctor. I did not allow Vernell to intimidate me and I recognized his judgement was altered from being high on drugs.

We gathered beside Momma's bed. Dr. Williams showed us an X-ray to explain what was going on. The medical photo was in color. It was a large, yellowish mass occupying most of Momma's body.

Dr. Williams' terminology was difficult to comprehend. I thought to myself, 'Is she saying what I think she's saying?' Finally, my sister and me pulled her aside to ask for clarity.

"Your mother has stage 4 colon cancer. The picture of this yellow object is a large tumor that has taken over most of her body," Dr. Williams explained.

Everything seemed to go in slow-motion as the doctor gave us the news of Momma's fate.

"So, what exactly does that mean?" Denise asked.

"With this being said, there is nothing else that we can do for her. Unfortunately, your mother is not a candidate for chemo or radiation. Her heart is not strong enough for any type of surgery. The most we can do at this point is to make her as comfortable as possible," Dr. Williams replied.

There was silence in the room. I looked at my sister Denise and my brother Vernell. Then, they both looked back at me puzzled. Momma just was gazing out the window.

"So, what other options do we have at this point?" I asked, desperately.

The doctor repeated her diagnosis. Slowly, we were processing the information that Dr. Williams had given us. She walked us out into the hallway.

"Well, as I stated, at this point there's nothing else that we can do for her with stage 4 cancer, except to make her comfortable. There are no other options," Dr, Williams said.

"So, what do you mean there's nothing that you can do?" Denise asked, with deep concern.

"It could be a week, it could be a month, or it could be six months. I'm not God. I can't say exactly how long it's going to be, but there's nothing else that can be done here for your mother besides to make her as comfortable as possible," Dr. Williams said, as she dropped her head.

I will never forget those words tucked away in the file of my mind. At that moment, instantly a light bulb came on. My sister gasped and her eyes appeared large as saucers. She let out a startling scream that could have woke up the dead.

"Oh, no, Momma!" Denise yelled. She took off running down the hallway, crying hysterically.

I chased after her. "Denise, Denise. Stop, come back," I pleaded.

Denise continued running towards the elevator. I rushed to the family waiting room to get her boyfriend Freddie to help me restrain her. I recall the hospital being terribly busy that day on the Oncology Unit. It was a dramatic scene. The staff and visitors were crowding around as onlookers. Denise slid down the wall collapsing onto the floor. I was trying to console her, but at that point it was nothing to be said. It was best to allow her to get it all out. Her boyfriend Freddie helped her walk back to the family waiting room. After a while she was able to gain her composure.

Shifting Gears

Although the doctor stated Momma's diagnosis, I still couldn't mentally process it. Accepting the news that my mother's life was coming to an end was unimaginable. I had witnessed God's healing power and experienced many victorious outcomes over the years. I told myself, 'Surely, God will do it for Momma.'

~There's Nothing Too Hard for God. ~

After things calmed down from the initial devastation, I walked back into Momma's hospital room to check on her. She was still laying there gazing out the window. While at her bedside I caressed her hand.
"Momma, did you already know that you were this sick?" I asked, concerned.
"No, not to this degree," she said, softly.

She turned back to the window and stared up into the sky.

My mother instilled in me that prayer was the key to every dilemma in life. She was such was a woman of faith. I wondered what was going through her mind. All of the sudden, Momma turned and looked at me with a sweet peace enveloping her.

"It's between me and God now baby," Momma said, soberly. Her words became few from that moment forward.

Momma was counting on me. I felt responsible to look after her. It appears I was operating outside of my body. I was not going to drop the ball. I began to monitor all the phone calls coming in from relatives and friends all over the United States.

My other siblings in California were waiting for an update about the meeting with the doctor. I had my own cell phone clipped on my right side, and Momma's cell phone on my left. Also, the phone in her hospital room was ringing nonstop. My mother had birthed eleven children: 8 boys, and 3 girls. One of my younger brothers died twelve years prior. Momma had over forty grandchildren, numerous great-grandchildren, and many friends. Everybody loved Momma!

I continued to pray with Momma and anoint her with blessed oil daily. Not once did I allow doubt to set in. I was in a spiritual warfare zone. I refused to believe Momma was dying.

My cousin lived in Atlanta; she was my mother's niece from her only brother Frank. Her name was Lucinda and she pastored a church. Her and Momma had become quite close over the years. Prior to this situation, I only met her once. Her and husband came to the hospital every day to check on Momma. Her support was a blessing. I knew that Lucinda had Momma's best interest at heart.

There was a female patient sharing a room with Momma in the hospital. From day one, she was so concerned about us. She overheard our conversations, prayers, and the diagnosis from the doctor. The next time I got ready to pray for my mother, the lady asked if she could join in. I consented, so she got out of her bed and stood beside Momma's bed. That woman broke out speaking in tongues.

Shortly after the prayer, the lady shared that she had no idea why a leg injury would place her on a floor with cancer patients. I knew this connection was all God. I automatically assumed she was a cancer patient too.

"I'll be going home soon. Can I give you my phone number, so I can call to see how your mother is doing?" she asked, sincerely.

"Absolutely," I replied.

I believe God had this lady there for support and prayer because He works in mysterious ways.

~ God truly is a keeper. ~

God Speaks

Waiting on instructions from the Lord, had me at a standstill. I felt like everything was in limbo. I stayed in prayer to remain undergirded by the Holy Spirit. My silent prayer was, 'Oh Lord, I truly believe you are going to heal Momma. I need to hear from you. Lord, what should I do now? The doctors are saying one thing, but what do you say Lord?'

I heard a clear, subtle voice.

"I am going to heal her. Not in the way that you think. But it is the ultimate healing. Your mother only has two days to live, and I am going to bring her home with me. Call your family and let them know they have two days to get here if they want to see her because she will be gone," the Lord spoke into my spirit.

I thought, 'What better way to be healed, than to go home to be with God!'

My spirit became excited and I was so thrilled for my mother! There was a peace that hovered over me that's indescribable. It was the type of peace that only God can give. Once God spoke, there was a release in my Spirit. I immediately accepted it. I did not question the voice of the Lord talking to me. My spirit bared witness. Without hesitation, I contacted my siblings.

Subconsciously, I was hoping no one misinterpreted my joy as morbid. I believed the glorious outcome that the Bible taught concerning, "life after death." God was taking Momma home to heaven. *"To be absent from the body, is to be present with the Lord"* (2 Corinthians 5:8). I thought to myself, 'Momma has been through so much, God knows what is best for her. She is getting ready to pass from labor to reward.'

Most of my siblings had a history of drug addiction, incarceration, and unproductive lifestyles. As a result of their struggles, their poor decisions affected Momma. Her codependency caused a few of them to move from California to Atlanta pursuing a fresh start. Over the years, as grown adults my siblings took advantage of Momma. Many had relapsed on crack cocaine. As a result, they stole from our own Mother while on crack binges.

The last time I visited Momma's house I was appalled. She had resulted to barricading herself in the house. Momma was trying to prevent any more theft. It was so sad that she had to live like that. On one occasion, I remember receiving a phone call from Momma as she stood by the front door, and one of my brothers was on a crack rampage. He was cursing her out because she wouldn't let him in the house. I was all the way in California unable to dash to her aid.

I shouted angrily, "Call the police!"

"No, no, no, she stuttered nervously. I'm just gonna wait for him to leave. I don't want the police to come hurt him."

I was furious and desired to move my mother into a senior citizen's complex in California.

The tumultuous incidents that occurred over the years were countless from most Momma's adult children. Once God spoke that He was going to grant her an ultimate healing, all I could think about was no more heartache, no more tears, and no more mistreatment. Several of my brothers had been addicted to crack cocaine and knew how to manipulate Momma. She suffered decades of emotional abuse, mental anguish, and disappointment behind her children. She would put them out, and somehow, they would end up right back in her house. The vicious cycle repeated. Momma called me and let off steam venting about their crazy escapades two to three times a week.

The Holy Spirit led me to tell my brothers Vernell, Price and sister Denise to individually spend time with Momma. And that it would be wise for them to clear their conscience through apologies to Momma for any heartache they caused in the past. I'm not sure if they understood the seriousness of what I was suggesting. Nonetheless, I obeyed God.

I left my mother's bedside to allow them privacy. My little sister Denise, who battled with a crack addiction for many years went in first. Thankfully, during this time she was clean. She spent some time with Momma and came out with tears streaming down her cheeks.

My baby brother Vernell entered the room after Denise exited. I could hear Momma chuckling at his jokes. He was the youngest of the eleven, and the tallest, standing at 6 feet 5 inches. He spent most of his life in and out of jail or disappearing on a drug binge. In the most difficult times, he knew how to get a laugh out of Momma. Vernell had been so far gone on drugs, he stole Momma's chitterlings and holiday feast out the freezer one year. Sadly, Momma was informed later that he exchanged the food for crack cocaine. He had been living with his girlfriend for about seventeen years.

My mother used to tell Vernell that God was not pleased with his actions. Momma always prayed for him to get his life together. Vernell made a promise to Momma on her deathbed. "I'm going to get married Momma. I promise you. I'm going to beat this addiction and my life is going to change," he said. My mother looked at him and smiled. I'm sure she had heard that line before.

Vernell told her a few more jokes, gave her a kiss, and walked out of the room.

Later that evening, my other brother Price who resided in Atlanta made his grand entrance. He could sweet talk Momma like none other. He had a beautiful smile that could charm a snake. Price was the type that took pride in his appearance. He loved being meticulously neat and wearing good smelling cologne. Although he too was hooked on crack cocaine you would not know it. People loved Price, and he could quickly bond with strangers. He loved to laugh, even when there was nothing funny.

There were still a few visitors in the room when Price arrived. He had a friend with him. I was watching and praying as each person came to visit. I could not come off my post.

"Hello Price," I said.

"Hey Sis," he replied, as he reached out to hug me.

"This is Pastor Brown, and I brought him to pray for Momma."

"Hello, Pastor Brown," I responded respectfully, as I shook his hand.

I never met Price's Pastor and was not sure what religion he was affiliated with.

"Excuse us for a moment Pastor Brown." I turned to Price. "Could I have a word with you out in the hall Price?"

"What denomination is Pastor Brown?" I asked.

"Oh, he's Apostolic Sis," Price replied.

I did not believe in allowing someone to lay hands or pray over my Mother that was not in agreement with our beliefs, especially not on her death bed. I was relieved as I walked back into my Momma's room for the prayer. Pastor Brown's prayer was anointed. The presence of God was in that room! Before Price left the hospital, he had his private time with Momma to make sure his conscience was clear concerning her. He was another treacherous thief who had cussed her out and kicked her door on his drugs binges.

All my siblings at one-time or another had been saved. At the time Ricky and Deon were the only two maintaining a relationship with God. The others were on two different pages opposing me. As I was flowing in the Spirit, they were operating in their flesh.

Humbly and thankfully, I had been consistent in serving the Lord over twenty years. My siblings were aware that God's hand and favor was on my life. I could discern that some of them did not agree with Momma putting me in charge. She had already made it clear what was to take place after her demise. Accepting her fate with a calm demeanor, Momma knew that as her eldest daughter her guidelines would be followed by me.

"I want to be buried in one of those white gowns at Goolsby funeral home."

"Yes Momma," I answered, attentively.

The next few days were busy. Everything moved so fast. I had already contacted my siblings. My two oldest brothers Wendell and Terrell were at our family reunion in our hometown Oceanside, California. They were saddencd to get the news about Momma.

Rick, brother number 3 was notified of the severity of Momma's illness. He had been fighting colon cancer for about 4 years. He was one of Momma's favorite sons. Rick bought Momma her first home in California back when his trucking business was flourishing. He was heartbroken that he was too ill to travel and be at Momma's bedside.

My mother was just in California visiting Rick the year prior. The strangest thing, she looked like the picture of health and we had no knowledge that she was sick too. Momma had come to see about Rick because the doctors said his condition was getting worse. If God did not intervene, Rick would not be with us much longer either.

Ross and Deon, brother number 4 and 6 were in California also. They scurried to make arrangements to get to Momma as soon as they could. My sister Yvonne, 4 years my junior, was just in Atlanta for Mother's Day 3 months prior to Momma's illness. She was having serious health issues, with blood clots in her legs. Yvonne's doctor had forbidden her to travel. She was devastated as well.

I had to forge ahead and put my trust in God. I began to cast my cares on Him and stayed strong for Momma. There was so much to tend to. The phones continued to ring off the hook. The word of Momma's illness spread quickly. The church members were calling and visiting. Her adopted sons and daughters that she bonded with over the years came to see her too. My cell phone, Momma's cell, and the hospital phone literally never stopped ringing. My niece Tanesha that Momma raised was expected to arrive from college any moment now. I called to check on her.

"Grandma is waiting on you baby," I said.

"I'm coming, auntie, as fast as I can." Tanesha replied.

Being on a scholarship required certain stipulations. It was the end of the college semester. Tanesha was completing her final exams. She was extremely focused and did not deviate from her goals. Even with all that was transpiring with Grandma, she had to handle her business.

Me and my sister Denise met with the social worker. Some referrals to a few locations for hospice care were given to us. We also had the option to send Momma home. Reality was setting in. My mother decided she wanted to spend her final days at her own house. We never had to make these types of decisions for a parent. I remained optimistic.

I don't think it had registered with my sister Denise that Momma was actually going to die in two days. She ordered all sorts of equipment to be delivered to our mother's house. However, the words God spoke to me, 'She'll be gone in two days,' were etched in my memory. I did not oppose my sister, although I knew we were not going to need all those medical supplies.

"I want my mother to have everything she needs and send it right away," Denise told the social worker, in a snappy tone.

She had an attitude insisting these items were necessary. I felt as if she was acting out of guilt, because there had been a little tension between the two of them right before Momma went to the hospital.

Denise ordered a wheelchair, potty chair, hospital bed, a walker, and tons of Depends diapers. I was thinking to myself, 'She's not gonna need all that.' I just remained quiet to keep down confusion.

Most of our time was spent at the hospital that week. Meanwhile, Tanesha arrived from college. Denise is Tanesha's mother. Me and Denise took her into the hospital chapel to pray, update, and give her the details about Grandma's condition.

After this brief meeting Tanesha was anxious to see Momma. As soon as we walked into her room, she climbed up in the hospital bed and gave her a kiss and began to stroke her face.

"Hey Grandma, how are you feeling?"

"I'm good shugga, how are you doing? I see you made it safe," Momma said endearingly. Tanesha was always so affectionate and caring. She had been raised by Momma since she was a toddler. While she spent her time alone with Grandma, she made a promise to complete college. That made Momma very happy.

I called my daughter Nichol in Los Angeles to notify her.

"Nichol, I need to let you know that Grandma is very sick." I went on to explain the doctor's diagnosis. "She won't be with us much longer," I said.

"Oh no! Where is she? I want to talk to her," Nichol said, as her voice cracked.

I passed the phone to her. They spoke briefly.
"I love you Grandma," Nichol emphasized.
"I love you too baby. You be good okay. Jesus loves you," Momma said, softly.
"Okay, Grandma. Goodbye," Nichol said, crying.

It was a shame that my daughter Nichol could not travel to Atlanta either. Due to being in a controlling lesbian relationship, she did not want to face an altercation with her girlfriend. I knew this situation was going to cause Nichol to numb herself with alcohol and drugs. She avoided family for years because she was of her lifestyle. She was a college dropout, drug dealer, and affiliated with gangs. Most of my family was clueless of her lifestyle. Momma had lived with me during Nichol's childhood years, so she was one of her favorite grandchildren.

Last Ride Home

I had been in Atlanta for only 4 days, but it seemed as though a month had gone by. The time came for Momma to be released from the hospital. We had to gather all her plants, cards, and balloons to take to her house. We waited for the ambulance driver to come get her. At this point, Momma was completely silent. I remained focused, so that I could follow the list of instructions that the doctor had given me. It was Friday afternoon, and Sunday would mark 48 hours since the Lord spoke to me that she would be transitioning in 2 days.

August 8, 2008, it was a hot, humid day in Atlanta. My brother Price decided to ride in the ambulance with Momma. I drove her car with all of her belongings. I arrived at her house and unloaded everything. The hospice care had already delivered the equipment that Denise ordered. There sat the wheelchair and the hospital bed was setup in her room. The Depends diapers were almost to the ceiling on Momma's dresser, and her potty chair was at her bedside.

Our family and neighbors were outside waiting to welcome Momma home. As I pulled off from the hospital the ambulance was in route directly behind me. Almost 45 minutes passed by since I had been at Momma's. I thought, 'She'll be pulling up any minute now.' I was becoming concerned; I called my brother Price on his cell phone.
"Where are y'all?" I asked.
"You're not going to believe this," he said, laughing.
"What is it?"
"The ambulance broke down on the freeway," Price said.
"You've got to be kidding me! How crazy is that? I have never heard of anything like this ever happening before!" I said, giggling.

It was ninety-five degrees. They had to order another ambulance to bring her home. I am so glad my brother was there with Momma. My poor mother. That sure was a day to remember.

There was a lot of preparation towards making Momma as comfortable as possible. She expressed to me that she just wanted a peaceful environment to rest. Momma didn't want all of her sons to stay at her house when they arrived. She knew that would be a recipe for disaster.

"No smoking, drinking, or gambling in here," Momma said, sharply.

My brothers could be a handful, especially when they all got together. From this point on, my responsibilities were intense.

Tanesha loved her grandma. Momma was her rock from childhood. Growing up she participated in dance classes, and all kinds of extracurricular activities. Momma spoiled Tanesha but made sure she was raised in church. She also had a private tutor and was a debutant. My mother even volunteered at Tanesha's schools from elementary up until she completed the 11th grade. Momma joined the Darnell Senior Recreation Center, and finally stopped volunteering when Tanesha started 12th grade.

My niece was my right-hand girl. Tanesha was willing to help with anything and wanted Momma to be comfortable too. The plain white sheets on the hospice bed were not cozy in Tanesha's opinion, so she purchased some mint green ones. My mother was weak, which caused her to be immobile. Tanesha did not weigh much; she was a small little thing. She climbed up in Momma's bed and held her forward while both of us together changed her bedding.

Surrounded by the emotions earlier, Denise did not want to prolong Momma's discharge from the hospital. She assumed that the prescription could be filled at CVS pharmacy by Momma's house. Later that night, my mother was in pain and the Morphine was running low. I rushed to the 24-hour pharmacy after midnight. To my surprise, they did not have the medicine in stock. Tanesha was at the house with Momma, while I went from store to store searching for Morphine drops.

I remember seeing a freeway exit sign to Atlanta Zoo. I started getting frustrated. The GPS App on cell phones had not been invented yet. I was completely in unfamiliar surroundings as a California native. My concern was for Momma to escape suffering and be able to relax. I remained level-headed and decided to wait until the morning to avoid getting lost. We had to stretch out her dosages to last through the night.

"I need my medicine baby," Momma said. I could tell that she was in discomfort, but she didn't make it obvious. Every hour, I began to administer the liquid morphine under Momma's tongue. The pains were coming more frequently. She did not scream, but she took deep breaths, and lightly moaned.

I realized that it was a poor choice of judgement to attempt to fill Momma's prescription at the local pharmacy by her house. I was grateful to God that through prayer he intervened for her to get through the night without being in any extreme pain.

"He giveth power to the faint; and to them that have no might he increaseth strength."
Isaiah 40:29 KJV

The next day, I was able to fill the prescription making sure we had enough to last. Four of my brothers were still in route from California to Atlanta. Three of them were on Greyhound buses, and the other booked a flight. They all hoped to see Momma before she left this Earth. Every opportunity they had; my brothers were calling to check on the status of our mother. You are never prepared to say goodbye to a loved one. 'She will be gone in two days,' is what I kept hearing in my spirit.

My mother's house was like a revolving door. I wanted to keep a Godly atmosphere, so I only listened to my pastors DVD'S or gospel music. During Momma's transition to heaven, ministry was transpiring. It dawned on me that God was going to get the glory out of Momma's situation. I was praying for various people; folks were receiving the Holy Ghost right in Momma's living room, speaking in tongues!

People were bringing tons of food over to feed our family. There were so many dropping off full course soul food meals. We had pot roast, chicken, pork chops, cabbage, mac & cheese etc. There were even cakes, pies, and banana pudding. It's a Southern hospitality tradition, they believe in cooking to show kindness.

Bye Bye Momma

It was Sunday morning; we were approaching day number two. I was bracing myself, since the Lord gave me the insight that Momma was transitioning in 2 days. She laid in the bed quietly. There were still numerous phone calls coming in from all over. Two granddaughters' in California, wanted to speak to Momma on the phone. She had not seen them in over twenty years because their dad kept them isolated when he won a bitter custody battle. They were my sister Yvonne's children that lived in Seattle, Washington. Now both of them were grown ladies.

"Hi, Grandma this is Kenya, and Veeta," they both said, crying hysterically.

"Hey baby, good to hear your voices," Momma said, softly in a low tone.

"I can't believe, I haven't seen you in like forever! And now you're sick, and I may never see you again Grandma," Kenya said, with a cracking voice.

"I love you Grandma," Veeta said, sadly.

"Don't cry baby. Everything is going to be alright. Just trust God. I love you; I have to go now. Goodbye," Momma said.

She passed the phone back to me and motioned her hand to insinuate that she did not want to talk anymore.

The doorbell started ringing early on Sunday morning. Momma's church members came by on their way to service. The neighbors, young and old, came over too. Little children from the neighborhood even knocked on the door. Mostly everyone referred to her as Grandma.

"I want to see Grandma," they said.

I was staying up late tending to Momma, amongst juggling other things. I asked my niece Tanesha and her boyfriend to go buy me a cup of coffee. One of my favorite pleasures was to eat breakfast and treat myself to a good ole' Grande bold blend of Starbucks. When they returned, I was relieved as I was looking forward to taking a break.

There was a house full of people. Shortly after my hot coffee was given to me, breakfast was ready too. Another friend of Momma's walked in with her daughter. I was still in my pajamas.

"Don't touch that coffee or eat anything. Della needs the Holy Ghost, pray with her!" the Lord whispered in my inner ear.

I thought I was finally going to enjoy a long-deserved cup of my favorite coffee.

Immediately, I went in the living room to greet Della. Momma mentioned months ago that Della needed to receive the Holy Ghost. I met her when I previously visited Atlanta for Mother's Day that same year. Me and my sister Yvonne, and Momma attending a taping for TBN with her. I felt like I had superpowers because the anointing was intense upon me. God was talking to me like he did with Moses and the Burning Bush (Exodus 3). I was hearing instructions so clearly from God it left me speechless.

"Hello Della."

"Hi, I came to see Mother Fisher. Is it ok, how's she doing?" she asked, worried.

"Momma is as well as can be expected, considering all that she's been through," I responded.

There were people sitting on the front porch, the living room, and standing around in the kitchen. My pastors' DVDs of him preaching were playing at a moderate volume. I approached Della and stood within her reach.

"You need the Holy Ghost. Do you want to receive it today?" I asked, without hesitation.

"Yes, yes, I do!" Della belted out, in a loud cry.

"Receive ye the Holy Ghost. Jesus loves you, and He wants you to be filled with His Spirit!" I proclaimed.

I laid my hands on her forehead and began praying. The power of God swept through that living room. Instantly, Della began to speak with other tongues as the Spirit of God gave her utterance. She was crying and rejoicing. It was powerful! I was praising God with my hands raised, and dancing around the living room with joy. Visitors were still coming in and walking straight to Momma's bedroom.

Della's daughter named Kara, started to shed some tears. She was a friend of my niece, Tanesha. "Do you want the Holy Ghost too?" I asked. At first, she declined by shaking her head, 'No.' Then, she could not resist the power of God! "Yes, I want it too!" Kara hollered. I called out for Tanesha to assist me. "Get me some tissue! Oh, and a fan" I said. The tears were flowing down Kara's face. Not long after, Kara was filled with the Holy Ghost on the couch speaking in tongues.

Della spoke in tongues for about an hour. As she was speaking, she got up and walked back to Momma's room. She laid hands on Momma and began to pray. Then she kneeled on the side of her bed. I will never forget, it was 10:00 AM. On Sunday morning.

Momma's Pastor, Bishop Ruffy and his wife came over to pray. He sang an anointed song to Momma. It was incredible! We all joined in. The room was filled with the presence and praises of God. Family and friends surrounded the bed. My cousin Lucinda that was a Pastor, was there with us too. Amid the anointing as tears streamed down Tanesha's face, she began to dance under the quickening Spirit of God. Miss Irby, my mother's neighbor, who already was saved came over while all this praise and worship was going on.

My 4 brothers: Wendell, Deon, Ross, and Terrell were still in route from California. They were desperately anticipating being with Momma during her last moments on earth. Due to financial restraints their only option was the Greyhound bus. My oldest brother Wendell called right in the middle of all the worship. He heard the glory of God on the phone. It touched his heart.

"Hey! What's going on. Who's there?" he asked.

I named all the people present as the praises continued to go forth.

"I'm almost there, I arrive tomorrow," Wendell said.

"Alright, we'll pick you up at the bus station. I'll see you soon."

Once things calmed down, I felt I needed to take a shower and relax. I could not seem to find the time. The neighbor Miss Irby was a powerful, little elderly woman. She came down the hallway and placed her right hand on top of my head praying in tongues and in English. I passed out under the power of the Holy Ghost. That was just what I needed. I felt refreshed in my spirit. I was able to go take a shower and regroup momentarily.

Momma's Last Breath

As the evening approached there were less visitors. I made sure Momma was comfortable. I continued to squeeze the Morphine drops under her tongue. Her pains were coming closer together, so I had to administer it more often. She was extremely sedated at this point.

I knew it was just a matter of time that Momma would be resting in the arms of Jesus. I was ecstatic, as I imagined Momma's entrance into the pearly gates of heaven! I thought to myself, 'What a glorious time that will be! No one will ever be able to hurt her again!' No more pain, no more suffering.

We sent somebody to pick up my brother Price that lived a few miles away. Our baby brother Vernell, had not been around all day. My baby sister Denise, and her boyfriend Freddie were there since earlier. Tanesha was on her way back from college;

she had made a turn-around trip to tie up some loose ends in Augusta, Ga. My 4 brothers on the Greyhound bus, were still in route from California.

    I stared at Momma with endearment, I gave her a kiss and whispered in her ear, "I love you," and exited her room. The house was quiet and peaceful. I poured some soup into a bowl and sat at the dining room table. I sighed with relief, 'whew,' finally able to sit down and eat. Denise and her boyfriend Freddie were getting ready to go home.

"C'mon bay bay, let's take one mo' last look at her befo we go," Freddie said. Denise's boyfriend spoke with a thick southern accent.

"Oh no! Momma, Momma!" Denise yelled.

    I hurried down the hall to her room. Denise was up in Momma's bed on all fours, straddled over her screaming. She opened Momma's eyelids with her index finger.

"Denise! What are you doing?" I said, compassionately.

I knew she was in shock, so I tried to calm her down.

"Momma! Momma! wake up!" Denise yelled.

"She's still breathing Yevette!" Denise continued yelling, franticly.
"Come on baby," I said, gently.
As I reasoned with her to come down off Momma's bed.
"She's still warm, I can feel her breath!" she said, crying.
"She's gone Denise, she's gone," I said.

~Momma took her last breath. ~

Her boyfriend Freddie stood there quietly looking and did not know what to do. My brother Price came in the room. He also stood in silence. We hugged Denise on each side to console her. Momma's head was dropped to the side, with her mouth slightly open, and a drip of saliva was coming down the corner of her mouth. This morning, the Lord filled Momma's friend Della and her daughter at 10AM with the Holy Ghost. Now, it was Sunday night at 10PM, August 10, 2008 and Momma went from Earth to Glory. What an eventful day.

We all stood there speechless for a moment. There was nothing else to say or do.

It was final, our mother was eternally sleep. I tenderly touched her forehead. There was such a calmness in the room. I just stared at Momma. I thought, 'Wow! God surely said, she'll be gone in 2 days.'
I took a deep breath, and said, "Goodbye Momma, I love you."

At that moment, I did not feel sad at all. My spirit was at such peace in God. I understood that Momma was in a better situation by going to heaven, so I did not shed a tear. I was genuinely happy for my mother. I cannot explain the way God was keeping me emotionally and allowing me not sorrow as those who have no hope (1 Thessalonians 4:13).

I used the landline to call my brother Rick who was battling cancer at home in Los Angeles. I had been keeping him informed with every detail since he was unable to be there. He was in a lot of pain when he came to the phone.
"Praise the Lord, Rick," I said, in a serious tone. (That's a religious greeting that means 'hello').
"Praise the Lord," he replied, calmly.

There was a pause.

"Momma's gone, Rick. We're waiting on the coroner to pick up her body now," I said.

"Okay, thanks for calling me. I want to stay on the phone," he said, moaning in pain.

Rick tried to hold back his emotions. I knew he was heartbroken. I continued to be strong for him. As children, we were inseparable and like best friends growing up.

I used my cell phone to contact my sister Yvonne that lived in Seattle, Washington. Unfortunately, she was very sick and regretful that she couldn't be there. She also wanted to stay on the phone until the coroner picked up Momma's body. They both wanted to feel apart. Wendell, Terrell, Ross, and Deon had not arrived in time to say goodbye in person. I dialed each of them to relay the news from another relative's phone.

Denise contacted our youngest brother, Vernell. By the time he arrived at the house, the coroners were preparing Momma's body to be transferred to the mortuary. He has been addicted to crack cocaine for decades. It appeared he had been abusing drugs all day. His eyes were big as a deer in headlights. They were just about to take Momma out in the body bag, and Vernell wanted to say his last goodbye.

The coroner unzipped the bag and pulled back the sheets. The same green sheets my niece Tanesha just purchased 2 days ago for the hospice bed. Vernell looked at Momma and did not say anything. He went into another room and fell on the bed crying.

I was going to fulfill Momma's last wishes as best I could. I wanted to prevent her house from becoming a motel, or a place to congregate and drink alcohol. I had all the information from the social worker about the steps to take after she took her last breath. I contacted the nurse to record the time of her death.

They removed Momma's body very discreetly. It was quiet on her dead-end street and seemed like time had stood still. I was glad that none of the neighbors came outside to spectate. We walked out to the curb behind the coroner and watched them put her body in the back of the truck. My siblings, Rick and Yvonne were still on the phone. We stared into the dark as they pulled off turning the corner. All five of us waved goodbye as they took her away. We went back onto the porch and sat there silently to gather our thoughts.

The Arrangements

Soon as I awakened Monday morning, I prayed for direction and fortitude. God is so amazing! It was no strength of my own, only His grace was carrying me. I had so much to do now to prepare for Momma's burial. Everything was moving at a fast pace. I bought a large, yellow, notepad to outline a list of duties.

My oldest brother Wendell, called for a ride from the Greyhound station. He was a day late from seeing Momma for the last time. As he entered the house, he put his suitcase down in the living room and walked directly down the hallway to Momma's room. Wendell stood in there for a moment quietly.

"Wow! Momma is gone. I missed her by one day," he said. We all took a deep breath. Wendell began to tell me, how he felt the presence of God, when he called us.

"Man— You all were singing and praising God, and it sounded like angels! A certain sound was coming through the phone, everyone around me on the bus could hear it!" Wendell said, with excitement.

"Really? Wow it was truly an atmosphere that prepared her heart to be at ease and take that sting out of death," I replied.

"Yevette, guess what happened? While on my way here I was praying to make it in time to say goodbye to Momma. I dozed off and 'something' woke me up. Momma literally came to me in vision. I saw her dancing in all white in her living room with 3 angels and twirling around in circles! She looked young like she was about thirty-five years old. Momma had a red curly afro. Then, when I said, 'Momma' her face came towards me very closely smiling with a beautiful glow, and whoosh she disappeared!" Wendell said.

"My God! That's powerful. Sounds amazing!" I replied, with excitement!

God is so mindful, to comfort my brother and allow his prayer to be answered. I began to rejoice and praise God. Although Wendell was unable to physically see

Momma, she came to him spiritually in a vision before taking her last breath.

There was so much to do that day. My niece Tanesha returned from college to help me make funeral arrangements. I made a call to inform Momma's Pastor Bishop Ruffy that she had died. I also wanted to share our plans and get his input.

"Where are you all planning on having Mother Fisher's service?" he asked.

"We are getting ready to check on a few places now. We would have loved to have it at her own church, but your sanctuary does not have enough space," I said.

"Keep me updated, meanwhile, I'll check a few places also," Bishop Ruffy said.

Momma initially got saved one Mother's Day in California while visiting my church in 1987. I had been a member over twenty years at Peace Apostolic in Los Angeles. Momma joined Bishop Ruffy's church when she returned home from her Mother's Day trip. She enjoyed the family oriented and close-knit ministry in Atlanta. They called her, 'Mother Fisher.' Momma had been saved for twenty years, but she had been an avid churchgoer from her youth. My niece was well acquainted with most of Momma's friends, so she was able to give helpful advice.

"Grandma knows lots of people, Auntie. We are definitely going to need a place large enough to accommodate the service," Tanesha said.

"Okay, well let's call a few places," I said.

We made appointments with several churches. They were either way too large, or not big enough. Some were available, but on the wrong date. Later that day I received a call from my mother's Pastor, Bishop Ruffy.

"How is everything going, did you find a place large enough for Mother Fisher's service?" he asked.

"We're still looking. There's a lot to do, and I'm feeling a bit pressured," I said.

"I think I found a place to hold Mother Fisher's Homegoing," he said.

Bishop Ruffy gave me an address, and we went to meet him to check out the church.

I was in an unfamiliar city. I did not have many connections in Atlanta. I thought to myself, 'If only I was in California, I would have the support of my Pastor, church family, and friends.' It was very awkward for me. My niece Tanesha, and my cousin Lucinda were a great help.

Most of Momma's family were deceased, except for one sister that we called, 'Aunt Fuzz.' She was the youngest of Momma's five siblings. Aunt Fuzz was a recovering alcoholic who had become sort of a hermit over the years. As she had gotten older her social skills diminished.

The main thing was, I had the Lord on my side. I could not have done this without Him. Tanesha and I called Goolsby's funeral home. We spoke with the owner Marie to let her know my mother had passed away.

"I am so sorry to hear of Lera's passing," she said.

"Thank you so much. My mother left instructions for me to contact you," I explained.

"Yes, we received her body already," she said.

My mother had a long-term connection with the funeral homeowners. She had used their services for some family members in

Atlanta over the years. This was a really sobering experience to sit with a funeral director and plan for "your mother" was surreal. At the time, looking back in retrospect —I was so happy to be able to do this for my mother. She left me details of everything she wanted. The main thing that she emphasized was being buried in the 'white gown' that Goolsby's funeral home provided.

Me and Tanesha were handling the business affairs. My niece stepped into a roll that I had never seen her operate in before. My mother did a great job raising her! Momma took Tanesha to church faithfully, which established a good foundation. It was her first year in college, and Momma's death affected her deeply. It was more to her like losing a mother. Now, was the time to throw Grandma's final celebration.

I was amazed how Tanesha conducted business alongside of me. She looked professional in her crisp white blouse, pearl necklace, high heels, and signature Michael Kors purse on her forearm. The funeral director Marie added up the expenses.

Tanesha quietly tapped her calculator to tally up the cost. She was right in sync with Marie. We signed the contract and were made aware of the items needed to dress Momma properly for burial.

"Grandma went out like a Holy Ghost gangster," Tanesha said, as we got in the car.

"Yeah, she never seemed afraid of death," I replied.

There was silence as we drove away.

My brother Wendell was at Momma's house receiving guests. We had some friends who were like cousins, that brought over full course meals. When there is a death, people are so generous. We had food enough to serve an army.

Della was sitting in front of Momma's house when we returned from making the arrangements. She had called earlier while I was at Goolsby's Funeral Home. She had a co-worker with her that wanted to receive the Holy Ghost too. I had never met this co-worker before, barely knew Della. I guess after her phenomenal encounter of speaking in tongues; she wanted others to get filled with the Holy Ghost as well.

I quickly shifted into ministry mode. Despite what was going on, God equipped me to still be able to pray with her co-worker. I delegated the extended family to help entertain the other guests. Tanesha and me went into her bedroom and closed the door. I began to read the scriptures John 3:1-7, Acts 2:1-4, and Acts 2:37-38. I wanted her to understand more about salvation, and the infilling of Holy Ghost. Tanesha was right there, being my little helper.

Della was so excited about her co-worker. We were collectively praising God and continued praying. The presence of God entered Tanesha's bedroom. It was incredible! The co-worker was so broken. Suddenly, the woman began to cry and stutter a few foreign sounds. The few words evolved into fluent sentences. She began to speak with other tongues as the Spirit of God gave her the ability. We all began to rejoice. Tanesha was crying, and I was clapping my hands saying, "Thank you Jesus!" Della was ecstatic. God did it once again!

We encouraged the lady to cherish this precious gift of the Holy Ghost. I gave her some scriptures to study concerning baptism. I advised her to go to an Apostolic or UPC church to be baptized in the name of the Lord Jesus Christ, as the book of Acts has documented. She left my mother's house rejoicing. Momma's death was not in vain.

There were people all over the living room and dining area as we exited from the bedroom. Momma's friends from the Darnell Senior Center brought more food, cards, and money to us. Many requested to have a full service for Momma at, 'The Wake.' There were so many people that wanted to express their love and gratitude for all the years of volunteer work Momma had done. This would shorten the length of her actual funeral, and everyone who desired to say acknowledgements. I had no idea that Momma meant so much to so many people.

They do things a little different in the South. Years ago, I was visiting Atlanta, and one of my cousins took me to a Wake. People usually kept the body in the house all night just before the actual funeral service. Then the family and friends came and just sat around until late. It was a bit strange, but that is how they did things in the South.

For Momma's Wake, we planned to host it at the same church her Homegoing Service would be held. We thought that would be a nice gesture. At the actual funeral celebration of her legacy, it would be impossible to let all those that she knew to speak.

My brother Terrell arrived the next day. He was on medication for his mental state. Terrell also had been struggling with a crack addiction, off and on for most of his adult life. There was always a crisis Terrell was facing. He had been in jail, or in several halfway-rehabilitation houses. Now, he was fighting a criminal case resulting in an altercation with his probation officer, who in return broke Terrell's hip attempting to calm him down during a routine visit. To defend his plea of insanity he had to take psychological medication.

Terrell was a bit spaced out when he arrived in Atlanta. He was not himself at all, but at least the prescription had him calm. We picked him up from the bus station. Terrell strolled down the hallway just as my brother Wendell did when he arrived the day before. He stood in the doorway of Momma's room and stared at the hospital bed that she took her last breath in. He rubbed his head and was speechless. I could feel the pain that he was experiencing. She died on Sunday night and he arrived on Tuesday.

"Um, um, um, Momma is gone," Terrell said, very somberly and exhaled.

He just stood there and looked at her room. That touched my heart. He turned around and came back down the hallway into the living room. I could tell he was in disbelief. Then, he went back down the hallway and looked at her bed once again. "Oh Momma," he said. Terrell walked outside to gather his thoughts.

When Terrell came back in, he began to tell us the story of how my Momma appeared to him say, 'Goodbye,' while he was on the bus. I was amazed! God's ways never cease to surprise me.

"Hey Yevette, you ain't gone believe this!" Terrell said.

"What?" I responded.

"While I was on the bus, Momma came to me in a dream, and said, 'goodbye,'" Terrell exclaimed.

"Wow! That's awesome! Momma came to Wendell too," I said.

Even though they were not actually here at her bedside, it was comforting to know that God allowed them to have closure. It happened just like God specifically said. Within 2 days, "Momma took her last breath."

Yevette Fisher

A Friend to the Rescue

While Wendell, me, and Tanesha were out looking for a church to accommodate Momma's funeral, Bishop Ruffy called. He wanted us to meet him at a church in the area. Ironically, it was the same location my baby brother's funeral was held twelve years prior. My mother attended this church years ago for a short period of time before joining Bishop Ruffy's church.

We walked around the sanctuary viewing edifice Bishop Ruffy suggested. The aisles were so narrow, I could not fathom the casket being able to fit. Then, Bishop Ruffy led us back into the fellowship hall. His wife, Gertrude insisted it would be simply perfect for the repass. They both seemed to be very persistent about using this church. It was apparent that it was not going to be the right place for Momma's funeral/repass. Since my niece was raised by my mother, I discreetly asked her opinion.

"Tanesha, is this church going to be a good choice for Momma's homegoing?" I asked.

"Auntie this place is not big enough, Grandma has lots of friends, she knew people all over the city at different churches, schools, and volunteer programs. This is absolutely not going to be large enough," Tanesha said.

Bishop Ruffy was trying to persuade me to use this church, which was his Overseer's ministry. His wife, Gertrude Ruffy was agreeing with him. The Ruffy's were close to my mother and they valued her support. For twenty years, Momma had donated so much money toward the building fund and was incredibly supportive of the ministry. They even had a plaque hanging in the church displaying her name in recognition for the contributions she made.

Wendell, Tanesha, and I agreed that this church was not the right place. Bishop Ruffy and his wife kept trying to convince me to hold the services there. Since I oversaw the arrangements, they were targeting my final vote. I was depending on Tanesha's knowledge and decided to allow her to make the final decision. The pressure escalated, so much to do, and so little time to do it. Our minds were unanimously made up.

"Thank you so much, Bishop Ruffy and Lady Gertrude, but we're going to keep looking. Tanesha feels this church is not large enough. We will get back with you and let you know what we came up with," I said.

All the sudden, Bishop Ruffy's wife Gertrude grabbed me by the arm. She demanded that we step outside to talk. Once she had me isolated her whole demeanor changed.

"Now listen, Bishop Ruffy suggested this church for a reason. This is his Pastor's church. What you need to do is take his advice and use this church," Lady Gertrude said, sternly.

The first lady Gertrude was furious. She pointed her index finger, her arms were flying around, those green eyes were turning red, and she was inches from my face. I could not believe that she would approach me in such an ungodly manner, while I was making arrangements for my Mother's Homegoing Service. I was speechless at how aggressive she had become. Her whole demeanor was hostile. I was in disbelief. There seemed to be another motive behind this outburst. I remained quiet, the peace of God seemed to silence and restrain me.

"Thou wilt keep him in perfect peace, whose mind is stayed on thee: because he trusteth in thee. Isaiah 26:3 KJV

Thank the Lord I was girded up through prayer and had been fasting. The Spirit of God was surrounding me with a hedge of protection. The fiery darts of the enemy were being intercepted. My brother Wendell, my niece, and the Bishop walked outside as our conversation ended. I was praying in my mind. I thought to myself, 'Lord, help me to say the right thing to this woman.'

"We decided this church is not big enough. Thank you, we will get back with you once we have made our decision. God bless you and Bishop Ruffy," I replied, kindly. We walked away with integrity.

The next day, a former member of the Ruffy's church stopped by Momma's to pay their respect. As we were conversing, I shared with them the experience I had with the Ruffy's. They said the reason they were so adamant about having Momma's Homegoing at that location was because they wanted to take an offering at Momma's funeral. They also shared with me he was known to do this on other occasions. That was ludicrous! Who does that? Bishop Ruffy felt that if the services were held at his Overseer's church, it would put them in a position to call the shots. It made more sense now why they eagerly wanted to have Momma's funeral at an establishment they could raise money.

There was a knock and a voice coming through Momma's screen door. "Hey girl," she said. "Laura, Girl here I come!" I yelled, happily. What a relief to see her smiling face after such resistance with the Ruffy's and all the warfare I was experiencing. The Lord sent me help! She flew from Los Angeles, rented a car at the airport, and reserved a hotel.

At the time me and Laura had been friends for about fifteen years. We supported one another through some difficult seasons in our life. Both of Laura's parents, and her mother-in-law had already passed. She walked right in volunteering to assist in any way possible. Laura always had a positive outlook, no matter the situation.

My niece Tanesha returned to her dorm for a couple of days to secure her scholarship for the following semester. Laura stepped right in to help me. It was a blessing to have my dear friend beside me for comfort.

My brother Ross arrived by bus on Wednesday. He missed Momma taking her last breath by three days. My mother left instructions while she was on hospice care. She already experienced Ross' short-fused behavior when he stayed with her years ago while residing in Atlanta. He could become combative and his understanding was not the best at times. I certainly did not want him to get anything stirred up while others were grieving, so we decided for him to lodge elsewhere.

When I relayed the message to Ross, he was upset. He used to live in Atlanta for over 20 years before moving back to Los Angeles the year before Momma passed. He had plenty of friends and family in the city that he could stay with. Reluctantly, he found a place to stay. My main concern was to fulfill Momma's last wishes.

By Thursday, everything had been finalized. My cousin, Pastor Lucinda had found the church to use for Momma's homegoing service. We also decided to have the repass at Lucinda's house.

We had forgotten Momma's dentures, so we had to take them at the last minute to the funeral home. It was hectic. They notified us upon arrival that the mortician had already sealed her mouth. When we viewed her body, she was gorgeous. I was nudging Laura during the family viewing.

"Laura, girrrlll that don't look like Momma," I said, whispering, with a smirk.

"Aww, Grandma looks marvelous," Tanesha said, as she touched her hair.

She appeared fifteen years younger. Momma looked so angelic I did not recognize her. If Tanesha approved, that's all that mattered to me.

Warfare

The opposition became more intensified, which is defined as spiritual warfare. The adversary tried to turn the fire up a notch. Some of my siblings accused me of plotting to steal my mother's life insurance check. My sister Denise allowed her boyfriend Freddie whom she barely knew to fill her head with a bunch of lies. Due to Denise and Vernell being out of the will of God, they trusted the voice of the enemy. Freddie told them I was untrustworthy and going to "Rip off" insurance money from all the siblings.

That rumor was so far from the truth. Momma already told me that the insurance policy would only be enough to bury her. She emphasized, that since many of her kids were on drugs for years and had stolen from her, they were not deserving of anything. She spent anything extra on taking trips.

The attacks against me began coming from everywhere. My brother Price came over asking to borrow Momma's car. When I refused, he acted irate and started using tons of profanity. He was an abuser of crack cocaine. Bishop Ruffy came over right away to diffuse the situation. The stronghold of addiction had Price's mind. I told him to leave or I would call the police. Bishop Ruffy begged me to put my phone away and calm down.

My oldest brother, Wendell went into my deceased mother's bedroom and rolled up a marijuana joint on her dresser. I felt that was very disrespectful. He knew what kind of life our mother lived as a servant of the Lord. Momma did not allow any smoking or drinking alcohol in her house. We got into an argument and I had to take authority over Wendell's rebellious spirit. Bishop Ruffy convinced Wendell to stand in unity with me as the oldest brother; to set the tone amongst the rest of our siblings. I adamantly let all of them know that there would be no smoking and drinking in Momma's house, and to go off the property with anything unholy.

Eventually, all my siblings decided to conspire against me. I was determined to follow the instructions Momma gave me on her deathbed. I gained strength to withstand all the attacks of the enemy through prayer, reading my Bible, and trusting in the Lord.

"No weapon that is formed against thee shall prosper; and every tongue that shall rise against thee in judgment thou shalt condemn. This is the heritage of the servants of the Lord, and their righteousness is of me, saith the Lord." Isaiah 54:17 KJV

It had only been 5 days since Momma took her last breath, but it seemed like weeks. All these challenges were an attack to distract. Finally, the pre-service, better known as the *Wake* was this same evening. We had ironed out most of our differences and decided to complete the burial of my mother with a mature posture.

Our last sibling, Deon arrived in Atlanta that evening. He flew in the same day of the Wake and came straight to the church. Deon walked in there wearing short pants, dress socks and walking and the heel of his shoes. He looked like an idiot. He had become Pastor since we had last seen him, we expected him to show a little more respect for Momma. Nevertheless, we welcomed him with open arms.

Some quarrels and misunderstandings had transpired within the family which spanned over a decade and caused unresolved bitter feelings. The twenty-one year's Momma lived in Atlanta; Deon never came to visit her. He was estranged from the family for quite some time. Most of us who lived in the same city had not seen him in years. Deon had not seen my mother years before she passed. He had only spoken with her on the phone from time to time. He did not even visit her when she came to Los Angeles. Momma had expressed her hurt by Deon's actions over the years, and now she had taken her last breath.

We all agreed not to resurrect any past issues with Deon. Our focus was to get through the Homegoing Service without any further incidents. My brother Rick had advised Deon to act sensible and not to create any division while he was in Atlanta.

Surprisingly, everything went well at the Wake. Ironically, my four brothers that travelled from California all had similar testimonies that they shared at the ceremony. Momma had come to all of them to say goodbye through a dream or vision while they were in route to Atlanta.

The owner of the funeral home showed us kindness by sending free limousines to transport us to and from the Wake. The ceremony was so beautiful and supported by so many that loved Momma. Her friends from the Darnell Center, had such endearing remarks. The Wake went on for a few hours. They brought pictures, cards, donated money, and told stories. It was very touching. I was thanking God, we only had one more day until the actual Homegoing Service.

Family Feud

It was terribly hot and humid that summer in Georgia. Apart from my brother Deon, everyone had arrived earlier in the week. All the arguments and confusion had calmed down. Although, none of us had seen Deon in years, we desired to keep the atmosphere peaceful. I just wanted to get through this weekend without any further chaos.

After arriving back to Momma's house from the Wake, everyone was in a good mood. My siblings thanked me for all the hard work to make sure Momma had a nice pre-service. They were very pleased. Tanesha was equally responsible for the success of the arrangements.

My brother Deon never came to Atlanta to visit Momma, so he had never been to 243 Napoleon Drive. That was my mother's address and we always referred to her house that way. As we entered the house, Deon began to look around with some type of weird amazement on his face. He walked down the hallway toward Momma's room.

"So, this is 243 Napoleon Drive." Deon said. He was gazing up at the ceiling and looking around as if he was in a trance. Once Deon walked back toward the living room, he repeated himself again. "This is 243 Napoleon Dr. Wow, what's going on in here? It feels thick in here,"

"What do you mean it feels thick in here?" Denise replied, confused.

"Give me some oil, I need to pray," Deon said.

Now mind you, Deon had become a 'Pastor,' since we last saw him and it appeared, he was about to usurp his authority. Three of my other brothers, Wendell, Terrell, and Ross were present. I was in the back of the house packing an overnight bag to go stay at the hotel with my friend Laura. As I came down the hallway, I could feel the atmosphere had shifted. I was curious to see where this random evaluation stemmed from.

"Everyone needs to form a circle to pray," Deon demanded.

"I don't want to pray with you because your attitude ain't right," Denise said, sharply.

"Go ahead and dismiss yourself," Deon replied, firmly.

Denise walked to the front door to leave, and she must have had a second thought. At that moment, it seemed like slow motion. She stormed back towards Deon like a raging bull! Denise slapped him upside his head and twisted it back so fast, all we could do is look. We were frozen and in shock. No one tried to stop her. I think secretly we were glad that my sister Denise attacked him. My brother Deon got what was coming to him. Nothing like big families, never a dull moment. That one was for Momma.

As soon as we exited my mother's house, we all jumped on our cell phones. My friend Laura from California called her husband to tell him the story. Immediately, I called my brother Rick to tell him. My niece called her boyfriend from college to tell him what happened. We were all in the car talking at the same time. I felt as though Momma was avenged for Deon's abandonment and all the years, he was angry in isolation. I could not get much rest that night from replaying the family feud in my mind. While the others slept, I went to the lobby to put some words together to say at Momma's funeral the next morning.

Laid to Rest

There's always some anxiety just before a funeral. Six days had gone by since Momma took her last breath. August 16, 2008 had finally arrived to formally eulogize her. To prevent sharing one bathroom, all the women stayed overnight at the Marriott Hotel. My brothers stayed at our mother's house.

The limousines were picking everyone up for the funeral from Momma's address. The neighbors and friends met us there also. Getting everyone boarded in the right cars and making sure not to leave anyone was a task. Only this time, I had to be the one to assign the seats and keep things running smoothly. My prayer was, 'If we could only get through this day.'

My mother's sister, Aunt Fuzz was in the family car with my younger sister Denise, my niece Tanesha and myself. There was a woman standing looking through the limousine window, motioning us to roll down the window. I did not know her, but I rolled the window down since she stood looking in as if she wanted to say something.

"I was told to get in this car with you all," she explained.

My sister Denise rolled the window back up without a response. We were sitting in front of Momma's house in the funeral procession having a meeting on whether this woman can ride in the family car. She was once married to my uncle Frank many years ago, and from what I understand he had been married at least 5 times.

"Grandmother did not even like her. They were not close at all Auntie, so she is not riding in this family car," Tanesha said, in a serious tone.

"Nope Lera didn't like her, she ain't ridin' in this car," Aunt Fuzz said with a southern accent. My sister Denise agreed and it was a known fact, if need be she would fight. To keep down confusion I directed the woman to ride with her daughter whose vehicle was empty.

It was a beautiful sunny day. Once we arrived, we marched into our designated seats. The church was filled with floral arrangements from numerous people. The choir sang one of Momma's favorite songs, "The Storm is Over Now." I rejoiced and ran all over that church. Most of the people that came on Friday to the Wake, returned for the funeral Saturday.

Many got up and gave remarks. I spoke about 30 minutes reflecting on Momma, and didn't realize until later, I had done "my own" eulogy. The funeral director fulfilled my request and hired a videographer. My brothers looked handsome in their blue suits and white gloves as they proudly were active pallbearers.

Momma's Pastor, Bishop Ruffy preached a great sermon. His text was from Psalm 39:4-6. He did a wonderful job with the eulogy as he spoke of her character and accomplishments; both naturally and spiritually.

"Lord, make me to know mine end, and the measure of my days, what it is: that I may

know how frail I am. Behold, thou hast made my days as an handbreadth; and mine age is as nothing before thee: verily every man at his best state is altogether vanity. Selah. Surely every man walketh in a vain shew: surely, they are disquieted in vain: he heapeth up riches, and knoweth not who shall gather them." Psalm 39:4-6 KJV

At the close of the sermon, we had the final viewing. The family viewed her body after everyone else did. Momma's Homegoing celebration was a joyous occasion overall. As the choir sang the last upbeat song, we were approaching her casket. As Momma requested, she was elegantly dressed in a long white, flowing chiffon gown from Goolsby's Mortuary. Her hair and make-up looked amazing. I envisioned Momma as an angel because her countenance exuded such tranquility.

I began to dance, dance, dance in the Spirit across the front of the church. One last Holy Ghost hoorah in honor of Momma. I had a flashback of others in her living room, speaking with other tongues during the last two days before she transitioned. Those souls were spiritually birthed as Momma was naturally expiring. Truly her life impacted so many.

My mother would have loved watching us saying farewell to her. As we all stood around her casket others began to crowd in surrounding us. This would be our final goodbye. As they closed the top of the casket my oldest brother Wendell was instructed by the funeral director to do what is referred to as, "tucking her in for the night." What a beautiful sight. One that will be etched in my memory for years to come.

~Goodnight Momma see you in the morning. ~

Aftermath

I was so exhausted from the non-stop activities from the time I landed in Atlanta. The ministering, funeral arrangements, and everything else that had transpired throughout the week was a task. The following morning, I felt like I could exhale.

I received a call that woke me up around 7 AM. One of my cousins was in a panic when I answered.

"Get up, get up! Turn on the news!" she said, alarming.

"What is it?" I asked.

"The church where Aunt Lera's funeral was held burned down last night!" she hollered.

I dragged myself out of bed and turned on the television. I flicked through the channels to find the news station. I was shocked to see the church that we just had Momma's funeral, not even twenty-four hours ago was up in smoke. I could not believe that church caught on fire.

"You have got to be kidding me," I said, puzzled.

The news was following an investigation about an arsonist that was setting churches on fire in the Atlanta Metropolitan area. The fire bug seemed to be targeting ministries that were predominantly black. I was so grateful that this did not occur on the day of Momma's Homegoing service. That was one less thing that I had to deal with. However, I was sorry that it happened.

Wedding Bells

Since my baby brother Vernell made a deathbed confession, I gave him a friendly reminder. As his big sister, I made a courageous suggestion.
"Hey Vernell, I have a great idea!" I said, excited.
"What is it sis?" Vernell asked, suspicious in a baritone voice.
"Why don't you and Karen get married while all your siblings are already here in Atlanta?"
"Hmph, ok I don't see why not. Let's get the plans into effect sis," he said.

At the time, it sounded convenient and honorable. Since he was still grieving, I think he was easily persuaded to "tie the knot" after seventeen years of living together. I hurried up and contacted Bishop Ruffy for an impromptu wedding. What a series of events: Momma was buried on a Saturday, the church burned down the next day, and now three days later we were having a wedding. Only in the crazy Fisher family. Denise apologized to Deon also for slapping him, and they made amends before he went back home.

Everyone was in support of Vernell and Karen's decision. We went down to the church on a Tuesday afternoon and had a wedding. We are all happy for them. After the wedding, we went back to their house and celebrated with cake and ice cream. Vernell claimed he was going to re-commit his life back to the Lord, and check-in to a drug rehabilitation program. Momma would have been so happy that he kept his promise.

A few weeks later it was as though they had never taken a vow. Vernell only stayed in church a few weeks and he never stopped abusing drugs. Karen end up kicking him out again as usual. The only good that came out of that, is he was true to his promise to Momma and got married.

Sweet Memories

Some of my favorite memories I recall about Momma bring joy to my heart. We shared so many good times it's difficult to condense these reflections into a capsule form. This is one of my favorites.'

One year in the spring, my good friend Laura and I flew to Atlanta for a church P.A.W. convention. My mother was so excited that we were coming to town. We drove straight from the airport to her house. She cooked Southern BBQ in her backyard, and we had a great time.

Momma enjoyed going to the Darnell Senior Center. She got dressed every morning as if she was headed to a full-time job. The place was a beautiful state of the art facility with an Olympic size swimming pool, TV lounge, sewing room, huge kitchen, and dining area. Besides going to church, the Darnell Center was her second favorite place.

She had lots of friends there that loved her. Whenever any of us came to town, Momma took us to meet her extended family.

Momma's church was the hospitality base that year for our national church convention. We were in the same denominational organization. She volunteered to work and was so proud standing in the lobby of the Convention Center. Momma had a black dress, with a beautiful lavender corsage pinned on her shoulder while directing the attendees toward the service.

Me and Laura hung out with my mother quite a bit that week. She adored my good friend Laura and considered her a surrogate daughter. "Make sure y'all make some time to come to the Darnell center," Momma said. It was a known fact how much she valued her friends and enjoyed her recreational hangout.

Momma thought we forgot our promise to visit the senior center after a couple of days. This particular morning, we picked her up she sat in the back-seat pouting. She didn't know we planned to visit the

Darnell center. It was the funniest thing. "Which way do we turn Momma?" The moment I asked; my mother perked up! "Oh, are we going to the Darnell center?" she asked. Momma's demeanor changed from silence to laughter instantly. She assumed we were headed back to one of the morning church seminars. That was an unforgettable, amusing moment with Momma.

We arrived at the Darnell Center for a grand tour. Momma introduced us both as her daughters. Several employees from the receptionist to the supervisor greeted us. The older men on canes and wheelchairs came out the woodworks to get a glance at Miss Lera's daughters.

The senior citizens looked at me, then back at Laura. My Mother got a kick out of that. My friend Laura has a light complexion, with long honey-blonde hair down her back; could easily pass for a white lady. My skin color is a caramel complexion, and my hair is a shorter length with a different texture from Laura. We have no similarities.

Momma had a great sense of humor and loved a laugh. The seniors were puzzled trying to figure out if my mother had dated a white man. Laura played along with the joke. "So, this is your daughter, Miss Lera?" they asked. "Mmmm hmm," Momma said. Laura has a bubbly personality, so she flirted with the old guys to boost their ego.

I was glad that Momma had a place that she could interact with people. She had many good times at the Darnell Center. They went on trips, had fashion shows, and luncheons. Everyone there loved Momma. She was scheduled to go on a trip to Alaska at the time she took ill.

After her passing, it was told to me that a supervisor at the senior center noticed Momma did not look well one day. She suggested to my mother that she should go get some rest because her skin looked pale. As her normal routine, Momma had driven herself, so the supervisor designated an employee to drive her home. Another employee followed them to give the driver a ride back. They had no idea that would be Momma's last visit to the center she loved so dearly.

Three months before my mother passed, I decided to go to Atlanta and spend Mother's Day with her. We had no knowledge that she had Cancer. This was the first time in twenty years that I spent Mother's Day in Atlanta. Normally, she would fly to the West Coast where most of the family lived. My middle sister Yvonne lived in Seattle almost twenty years and had never been to Atlanta, so I bought her a ticket to meet me there. My baby sister Denise was already staying in Atlanta at the time.

My plan was to have a "girl's day" with my mother and her daughters. I was anticipating this reunion. We were distant in age and had not all been together in years. I envisioned us having a good ole time in the Lord. That week was so far from what I imagined. It truly was a Mother's Day to remember.

My mother and sister Yvonne were constantly at odds with one another. My youngest sister Denise, was angry with Momma over, "who knows what." Their indifferences had gone on back and forth for over twenty years. As the oldest daughter I always tried to be the peacemaker. We had no idea that Yvonne was on antidepressant medicine called Paxil. Denise was recovering once again from her drug addiction. I guess she was having some sort of withdrawals, so she was in a strange space in her life.

I had been living as a devout Christian for about twenty years. Though we had the same mother and father, our personalities were totally different. I was willing to overlook any differences to happily celebrate Mother's Day. We had plans to take glamour head shots together. That was popular during that era. Well, let me tell you, that never happened.

Saturday morning, as we prepared to go to the photo studio my sister Yvonne had a meltdown. I had not been in her company in over 10 years, so I didn't know what was going on. I went to tell her that we were ready to go, but instead found her sitting in the middle of the floor in a pile of clothes dumped out of her suitcase. Yvonne was crying uncontrollably. I tried to console her. However, I had no knowledge as to what the problem was.

"What's wrong with you Yvonne?" I asked.
"I don't know," she said, hysterically.

My sister Denise came in and got down on the floor attempting to calm Yvonne down. It was insane. The plans I made were not going well. I did what I knew to do best, which was go into prayer. I got my Blessed Oil and gathered everyone in Momma's living room. I laid hands on both of my sister's foreheads and they fell out speaking in tongues.

Momma with her funny personality, looked over at me grinning. "Lay hands on me too Yevette," she said. She loved feeling God's anointing power. She too passed out on her living room floor! A sweet peaceful presence entered the room. We ended up taking photos on a digital camera at Momma's house and getting them developed at CVS' photo department.

It had later been told to me that Yvonne was also upset about my brother Vernell vanishing with her last $25 to buy marijuana. She had hopes of smoking weed, instead of the meds to calm her nerves. I was so amused once I found out this fiasco was the cause of our family portraits being cancelled. Whatever dilemmas we faced; we could always laugh about it after the fact.

My mother was treating us as if we were still little girls. All we could do at this point was to grit and bare it. Since we only were going to be together for the week, I knew her bossy demeanor would not last forever.

Momma had a list of events planned for us. Her friend gave us some tickets to Trinity Broadcasting Network (TBN). The same morning of the taping is when she told us we were going. I personally had no interest. Once I discussed it with my sister Yvonne, she did not want to go either. My youngest sister Denise refused and made it clear that it was not up for discussion.

As for me and Yvonne, our mother would not take "no" for an answer. She insisted we put our clothes on like good little girls and get in the car. We felt forced since we were staying at her house.

"Hurry up and get dressed. Miss Greenie will be here any moment," Momma said, happily.

Unbeknownst to us, it was 2 carloads of people that were going on this escapade. My sister and me had been bamboozled. We changed our attitude along the ride as we jokingly gestured to one another. By the time we got to the television station, there were about 10 people in our party.

Surprisingly, we had the best time of our lives. We enjoyed the singing, preaching, and fellowship. I had travelled over 1,200 miles away from home to visit a station that was only thirty minutes outside of Los Angeles. That was my first trip ever to TBN. We even received these large souvenir mugs with their crest on it. They gave us a tour of the station, which included all the beautiful rooms that were set up for tapings. I cherished that cup for many years.

Afterward, we all went to the Red Lobster for dinner. Yvonne was reminiscing on the night, while enjoying the delicious seafood. "It's a beautiful thing, it's a beautiful thing," Yvonne said. That was her phrase for 'this is awesome.' We laughed so hard when she said that.

The duration of the week Momma took us to the Darnell Senior Center for lunch, and another day she took us back for a fashion show. Then, she took us to the Olympic Park downtown Atlanta, and on a tour of Martin Luther King's old house. We ate at a soul food restaurant called, "Beautiful." The food was delicious! We had a fantastic time.
"It's a beautiful thing, it's a beautiful thing," Yvonne said, repeatedly.

My sister Yvonne flew back to Seattle 2 days later. My mother finished off our 7-day reunion with a dinner-suspense play. She promised another buddy from the senior center, that we would go so that she could do something nice for me. This was a play where you had to guess who had committed the crime. My Mother's friends loved her and wanted to be kind to her family visiting from out-of-town.

My sister's slogan became quite catchy after that Atlanta trip. We used that saying in reference to Yvonne from that day forward. Truly it was a "beautiful thing," in spite of all that transpired Mother's Day 2008.

I ended up staying in Atlanta with Momma for about a month. I came on a buddy pass and could not get a flight out right away. Overall, we had a good time. I had no idea, that would be the last occasion all of us would be together with Momma. Three months later my mother passed away from stage 4 Colon Cancer.

She never breathed a word to anyone, but later we found out Momma had been sick for at least seven years. Denise had been trying to express to me for years that she felt like something was wrong with Momma. I thought my sister was delusional on drugs. Prior to Momma's death, God sent a prophet that called me. "Get your mother's house in order," he instructed. I had no idea he was speaking of her spiritual house. Instead, I began to eliminate clutter in her home.

Reflections of our Bond

We were raised in a small town in Oceanside California, in the late 1950's. I never met my grandparents, Lillie Mae and Frank Reid. My mother never met her own father, and she was told he died from hiccups. I recall when I was around 6 years old during Christmas, Momma had to take a train down South to her mother's funeral. She could not afford to bring anyone with her. All my siblings were left with various family members until she returned. We did not have our typical celebratory holiday that year with gifts, a tree, and soul food.

Momma talked about the untimely death of her twin sister on many occasions. Her name was Leah, it would make me sad as a little girl when she reflected on memories of her. She seemed to never have healed from losing her twin.

My parents would often get into heated arguments and separate. Momma would gather the children and temporarily move with relatives. Daddy would somehow come find us within weeks. Then, we would go back, they would make up, and the babies kept coming. Both of my parents always worked a lot. Being the oldest girl and third oldest child, I was responsible to take care of my siblings.

I recall an incident in the third grade when I came home from school, Momma had our belongings packed. Some things were in suitcases; the remainder of items were in trash bags. Momma called a taxi to drop us at the train station. Once we got there, she realized that some money orders were left on the dining room table. Momma was frantic because she needed that money to support us. My two older brothers Wendell and Terrell were around ten and eleven years old, so she left them in charge of my other seven siblings. Momma took me back with her to retrieve the money orders.

The train was not scheduled to depart yet. I remember walking in the house and to our surprise my father was home from work early. Momma quickly grabbed the money orders without saying a word.

"Lera, where are you going?" he asked.

As we exited, my father stood there looking puzzled.

"Lera, what is going on, where are you going?" Daddy asked again.

We walked out the front door and back up the street. She held my hand tightly. I remember looking back at my father thinking, 'What is going on?' A woman that we did not know gave us a ride back to the train station. That would be the last time we moved away from my father in Oceanside. From that day forward, I became my mother's closest friend. Prior to that I was her only friend. A year and a half later, Daddy came to Long Beach, California and moved in with us.

Coming up, Momma always took us to church every Sunday. Me and her remained close until I turned about fifteen. We became emotionally distant for a short period. I started to rebel against Momma during my teenage years after I found a strong interest in boys. She stayed right by my side until the phase passed. Momma used extreme measures of discipline by hitting us with tree branches, so I was afraid to disrespect her. Whatever she did not approved of, I tried to hide it from her. She seemed to know everything about her children anyway.

My Father had an affair with some strange woman. After twenty-five years of marriage and eleven children later, my parents finally decided to divorce. The verbal abuse was equivalent to physical, which probably prompted Momma to escape after discovering the infidelity. They had a turbulent relationship for almost twenty-five years. Momma kept the last name Fisher instead of her maiden name Reid. I was a senior in high school at the time and she made sure I was able to keep up with the latest fashion trends so that my senior year would be special. My two sisters were ten and four years under me.

Daddy later married a woman named Albertha. She was not attractive, overweight, had never been married, and had no children. My stepmother was a nurse. It was obvious to me and my siblings, Daddy married her for financial stability. When we visited our father, it was no secret he had his own bedroom. Albertha slept in another part of the house.

My childhood sweetheart and I conceived our daughter after high school. Momma was one of my first babysitters. She later became grandmother to several and loved all of them dearly. Momma cooked collard greens and tomatoes out of her garden. She had a house full of grandkids on the weekend and fed them grilled cheese with bologna sandwiches. They could run wild at her house.

As I got older, I spent lots of time talking to my mother. I thought she would reveal the mysterious man that caused her to move to California, but she never did. That's one secret Momma did not disclose. The only hint she gave me, was that he was a professional boxer. Throughout the years I understood Momma's life more in depth and felt her pain. I believe because I was her oldest daughter there was a special unbreakable bond that we shared. We also had a love for the things of God.

Momma did not have an opportunity to truly live her life to its fullest potential. She had been a wife and mother for over twenty years. After her divorce at forty-two, I talked her into going out on the town with me. I dressed her in some "hot pants" and a pair of thigh-high boots. We went to a bar, but she did not drink alcohol. She just wanted to have a little fun for once. Momma smoked long, slender brown Virginia cigarettes for years.

No matter what went on in our lives we remained close friends and confided in one another. Momma was full of wisdom. She loved the Lord and went to church every time the doors opened. Church was her life she also enjoyed singing in the choir. Momma also believed in the power of prayer and raised us up to embrace Christianity.

Later in her life she got the revelation of the full gospel (Acts 2:38). Momma received the infilling of the Holy Ghost and submitted to water baptism in the name of Jesus Christ while visiting me for Mother's Day. The Holy Ghost empowered her to stop smoking cigarettes. Whenever we went to church together, we would take off running in two separate directions praising the Lord! She loved being in an anointed atmosphere. And fellowshipping with believers.

My mother had an endearing personality. She loved to laugh, entertain people, cook, and travel. Momma was the pillar of the family. I learned a lot of morals and conduct from her honest lifestyle. Her life was simplistic in her old age. She found pleasure in going to church and spending her latter years at the Darnell Senior Center. I know that the only thing that got me through this difficult time was the faith in God and his word.

I can still hear her voice echoing in my thoughts, as though it was yesterday. When we are young, time goes by so fast. I don't think it really dawns on us that our parents won't be with us forever. Therefore it's so important to value every moment with them while they are with us. We must apply the wisdom they instilled in us and cherish their memories once they're gone.

Most assuredly, if I had not been filled with the Holy Spirit, there is no way I could have successfully managed the loss of my Mother. As I utilized my prayer language, the will of God was interceding on my behalf. The adversary cannot decode speaking in tongues, so it was an inner peace that rested upon me through this difficult period.

There is a time for everything, and a season for every activity under the heavens: ²a time to be born and a time to die, a time to plant and a time to uproot, ³a time to kill and a time to heal, a time to tear down and a time to build, ⁴a time to weep and a time to laugh, a time to mourn and a time to dance, ⁵a time to scatter stones and a time to gather them, a time to embrace and a time to refrain from embracing, ⁶a time to search and a time to give up, a time to keep and a time to throw away, ⁷a time to tear and a time to mend, a time to be silent and a time to speak, ⁸a time to love and a time to hate, a time for war and a time for peace. Ecclesiastes 3:11-8 NIV

Words of Encouragement

I have experienced numerous deaths in my family, so I know losing someone dear to you can be devastating. My beloved Mother's legacy leaves my heart filled with great memories. Even after Momma passed my brother Ricky, Price, and sister Yvonne also went home to be with the Lord. Family dynamics can become complicated, but there is a saying, "Blood is thicker than water." Suffering a loss can take you on such an emotional roller coaster, but remember God is our very present help in the time of trouble (Psalm 46:1). Without trying to intervene or work through your grief, allow time to be the healer.

We must take into consideration that after we have lived, one day we will die. *"It is appointed unto men once to die; but after this the judgement"* (Hebrews 9:27 KJV). But where will our soul spend eternity?

Knowing the Lord is so important as we face calamity, loss, or a rough season in life. The strength that God imparts is indescribable when you establish a personal relationship with Him.

Obeying the Plan of Salvation to secure your eternal resting place is a decision to make while you have the opportunity. Jesus emphasized in John 3:5, *"Truly, truly, I say you must be born again of the water and of the Spirit or you cannot enter into heaven."* The fulfilment of this mandate is found in the book of Acts after the Holy Spirit was poured out on the Day of Pentecost. *Peter said, "Repent, and be baptized every one of you in the name of Jesus Christ for the remission of sins and you shall receive the gift of the Holy Ghost"* (Acts 2:38 KJV).

The five phases of coping with death: denial, negotiating, anger, depression and acceptance help us identify what we may be feeling. Everyone may not experience all of them in a specific order. Perhaps with these stages you will retain insight of grief's obstacles, making you more knowledgeable about recovering from loss.

"I can do all things through Christ which strengtheneth me." Philippians 4:13 KJV

Denial is a defense mechanism that helps process your feelings of grief in increments. As time progresses, the feelings you avoided confronting begin to surface. After a loss, guilt is often intertwined with negotiating. The devil will cause us to find fault in ourselves and what we think we could have done differently. We remain in the past, struggling to maneuver our way through the hurt. Anger is a normal emotion after the death of a loved one. You may feel like God has abandoned you.

"May your unfailing love be my comfort, according to your promise to your servant." Psalm 119:76

The layer beneath anger is your pain. Depression can begin to weigh on you so heavy, that it feels as if it may never leave. If grief is a process of healing, then depression is one of the many emotions you may struggle with as well. Allowing the mountain of grief to run its course is essential before you begin to exuberantly thrust forward. It is never wise to oppress what needs to be addressed.

~Talking to a therapist is beneficial while compartmentalizing these feelings. ~

It is vital that you don't allow a *"spirit of grief"* to overtake you. What I mean by this is to the point that every time your deceased loved one's birthday or annual memorial comes around you sink into a depressive state. Satan wants to steal our "joy and peace of mind," which the Bible states our strength relies on. This demonic oppression must be renounced in the name of Jesus! <u>Acceptance</u> is about embracing the reality that your loved one is gone and functioning in their absence while celebrating their memory.

"So do not fear, for I am with you; do not be dismayed, for I am your God. I will

strengthen you and help you; I will uphold you with my righteous right hand."
Isaiah 41:10

<u>PRAYER</u> "Be merciful to me, Lord, for I am in distress; my eyes grow weak with sorrow, my soul and body with grief. My heart is broken, and all my tears are in your bottle. Jesus, you said, 'Blessed are those who mourn, for they will be comforted.' Please Father send me Your comfort now. Send angels of mercy to me. I need the peace of God, which transcends all understanding to guard my heart and mind. I ask for peaceful sleep, thoughts, and emotions to rule my days and nights. Lord, the Bible says, 'You are close to the brokenhearted and you rescue those whose spirits are crushed.' Draw close to me and help me not to grieve like those who haven't discovered your kindness and mercy. Help me to believe that tomorrow will be better, and the next day will be easier. I renounce the demon of grief that will cause my joy to be consumed in sadness. Lord I

know you will soothe my hurt with your balm in Gilead. In Jesus name. Amen."

~The Lord will keep you through every circumstance in life. ~

Yevette Fisher

Momma's Legacy

Lera Reid was born an identical twin on December 4, 1931 in Atlanta Ga. to Frank Reid Sr. and Lillie Mae Reid. For some strange reason, her mother Lillie Mae did not give her a middle name. Her twin was named Leah. Her other siblings were Frank and Elizabeth, which were older, and a baby sister named Margaret.

Lera grew up in Southwest Atlanta, where she attended Walker Elementary. She was brought up in Mt. Moriah Baptist Church. Her twin sister Leah died during their senior year of high school from an enlarged heart. The medical technology had not advanced to treat the diagnosis. Despite the devastation of losing her identical twin, Lera graduated from Booker T. Washington High School in 1949.

At the age of nineteen, she met a mysterious man in California. At some point,

Lera decided to move from the South by herself to start a new life. She never disclosed the name of the man she initially came to California to meet. Apparently, things did not work out between them. Once arriving in California, she got a job at Camp Pendleton Marine base in Oceanside, California.

At the age of nineteen while working at the Marine base, she met Price Washington Fisher. In 1953, at the age of twenty-two she was united in holy matrimony becoming Mrs. Lera Fisher. They had eleven children together by the time she was thirty-four years old. To this union were conceived, eight boys and three girls.

After being married over twenty years her marriage ended in divorce. She resided in Compton, California, until 1986 when she moved back to Atlanta to take care of two elderly aunts. While visiting her daughter Yevette on Mother's Day, Lera Fisher was baptized in the name of Jesus and received the precious gift of the Holy Ghost on May 10, 1987. She was *Born Again* (Acts 2:38) at Peace Apostolic Church in Carson, Ca. Upon her return to Georgia, she joined First

Apostolic Ministries where she was awarded Mother of the Year in 2007.

Mother Fisher, (as everyone referred to her) was a dedicated Grandmother. She took the responsibility of raising her youngest daughter's child named Tanesha. Lera took pride in her grand-daughter's scholastic achievement and tried to provide the best upbringing possible. She received numerous plaques, and awards for her dedicated service at the schools Tanesha attended.

Lera was involved in a plethora of activities. She volunteered at the Metro Atlanta Christian School and Adult Daycare. Lera had memberships with the Travel Club, Red Hat Society, Quilting Club, Counsel in Aging, and the Darnell Senior Center. She also sang in the choir. Mother Fisher was the voice of welcome that greeted everyone with a hug, kiss, a bag of assorted candy and smile. I loved Momma so much, but Jesus loves her more, and took her from labor to reward. She no longer had to suffer from Colon Cancer. The fact that my Mother was born again (John 3:5, Acts 2:38) qualified her to rest in the bosom of Jesus.

She will be missed by all her children and grandchildren. Her loving smile, the sound of her laughter and her witty sense of humor. The smell of coffee brewing and that thick crisp southern bacon cooking as you entered her home, are some of the memories I have of my dear sweet Mother. As a child, I can recall her love for God. Momma stayed on her knees praying for her children, and constantly reminded us how important is was to develop a relationship with God.

"Brothers and sisters, we do not want you to be uninformed about those who sleep in death, so that you do not grieve like the rest of mankind, who have no hope."
1 Thessalonians 4:13

www.ingramcontent.com/pod-product-compliance
Lightning Source LLC
Chambersburg PA
CBHW070500100426
42743CB00010B/1702